ACCESS

Building Literacy Through Learning ™

English

Assessment

EDUCATION GROUP

A Division of Houghton Mifflin Company

Credits
Development: Michael Priestley
Design and Production: Creative Pages, Inc.

The editors have made every effort to trace the ownership of all copyrighted selections found in this book and to make full acknowledgment for their use. Omissions brought to our attention will be corrected in a subsequent edition.

Photo Credits for Cover
Foreground: Backpack, © Photodisc/ Getty Images; Library Shelves, © Photodisc/ Getty Images *Background:* Photodisc/ Getty Images; BrandX/ Getty Images; Based on a system of labeling the columns A through J and the rows 1 through 18, the following background images were taken by the following photographers: A3, A5, A7, A9, A10, A13, A18, B1, B2, B4, C4, C5, C10, C11, C13, C17, D1, D3, D6, D7, D9, D14, D16, E4, E5, E7, E10, E12, E13, F4, F6, F9, F10, F17, H5, H17, H18, I1, I3, I4, I6, I12, I17, J4, J5, J7, J8, J9, J10, J12, J13: Philip Coblentz/ Getty Images; A16: Sexto Sol/ Getty Images; E9: Albert J Copley/ Getty Images; F1, J3: Steve Allen/ Getty Images; G7: Spike Mafford/ Getty Images

Photos: (Referenced by page-item#) pages 13a,c,f, 15c,f, 16c-e, 43a,b, 44b, 44e, 45b,d,e,f, 46c,d © Corbis

Illustrations: Drew-Brook-Cormack

Printed in the United States of America

ISBN 0-669-51657-0

1 2 3 4 5 6 7 8 9 10 — BA — 09 08 07 06 05 04

Contents

OVERVIEW

ACCESS: Building Literacy Through Learning is a program designed for middle school students who are English language learners. Instruction in this program emphasizes both subject area content—Reading and Writing—and English language skills. To help teachers and students use this program most effectively, this book provides a set of tests to accompany the *English* text. These tests are designed for use with students at varying levels of English language proficiency.

There are three kinds of tests in this book, as described below: the Pretest, Lesson Tests 1–24, and the Posttest. The Pretest and Posttest emphasize English language proficiency in the context of Reading and Writing. The Lesson Tests focus mainly on the content taught in the lessons.

The *Pretest* is designed to be administered at the beginning of the school year. This test has 36 items organized in three parts: Part 1: Vocabulary, Part 2: Grammar, and Part 3: Reading and Writing. Each part has 12 multiple-choice questions. The vocabulary words, grammar skills, and history and geography content in this test are drawn from the material taught in the textbook. The Pretest can be used for three purposes:

- to help you determine each student's level of English language proficiency and familiarity with basic concepts of Reading and Writing;

- to help you determine what language skills and background knowledge you might need to emphasize in your teaching; and

- to provide a baseline for measuring students' progress from the beginning of the year to the end.

The *Lesson Tests* in this book are designed to be used after each lesson to determine how well students have learned the lesson content and related vocabulary. Each Lesson Test is one page long and has 6 multiple-choice questions. The first question in each Lesson Test measures vocabulary knowledge with words and definitions drawn from the vocabulary taught in the lesson. Questions 2–6 measure the content of the lesson, emphasizing the Big Idea, Key Concepts, and Skill Building outlined in the "Talk and Explore" section of the lesson, the content information in the "Look and Read" section, and the comprehension strategy in the "Develop Language" section. To the extent possible in each lesson, the skill focus and comprehension strategy are embedded in the content questions.

The *Posttest* is parallel to the Pretest in structure and content. It should be administered at the end of the year to help determine how much progress students have made.

Directions for Administering Tests

To administer a test, make a copy of the test pages for each student. Then follow these guidelines.

- Plan on 45 to 60 minutes for administering the Pretest or Posttest and about 15 minutes for each Lesson Test. Give students more time if needed to accommodate differences in language proficiency. (Depending on your students, you may want to administer the three parts of the Pretest at different times.)

- Have students write their name at the top of each page.

- Read aloud the directions at the top of the first page of the test and make sure students understand what they are expected to do. Have students mark their answers on the test pages by choosing the best answer to each question and filling in the bubble beside the answer they choose.

- On the Pretest and Posttest, read the directions at the beginning of each part. At the top of the page for Part 1 and Part 2, you will see a *Sample* question with the answer bubble filled in. Read the sample item aloud and have a student provide the answer. Then show students how the answer bubble has been filled in to indicate the answer chosen. Make sure students understand what to do before proceeding.

- Monitor students as they work through the tests. If students appear to have significant difficulty understanding the test and answering questions, administer the rest of the test by reading each question aloud.

Directions for Scoring Tests

To score the Pretest and Posttest, refer to the appropriate **Answer Key** for the test (on pages 8-11) to check each student's answers. Circle the number of each item answered correctly. Draw an X through the number of any item answered incorrectly. Then count the total number correct and write the result in the *Score* box at the end of the test. (For the Pretest and Posttest, you may also want to count and record the total number correct for each part.)

To find the percentage score for a test, divide the number correct by the total number of questions on the test. For example, 27 correct out of 36 questions = 27/36, or 27 ÷ 36 = 0.75, or 75%.

For Lesson Tests, score each test in the same way. On a Lesson Test, students should answer at least 4 of 6 questions correctly (67%) to attain a passing score.

On the next two pages of this book, you will find an Individual Scoring Chart and a Class Record. Use the *Individual Scoring Chart* to record a student's scores on all English tests administered during the year. This chart can be used to help monitor and report on the student's progress during the year. Use the *Class Record* to document the Pretest and Posttest scores for all students in the class. This chart can be used to compare test results, to help determine and report on the students' progress from the beginning of the school year to the end, and to document how many students showed progress in English language proficiency.

Student name _____   Grade _____

Teacher name _____   Class _____

Assessment	Number Correct	Percent Score	Assessment	Number Correct	Percent Score
Pretest			Posttest		
Lesson Test 1			Lesson Test 13		
Lesson Test 2			Lesson Test 14		
Lesson Test 3			Lesson Test 15		
Lesson Test 4			Lesson Test 16		
Lesson Test 5			Lesson Test 17		
Lesson Test 6			Lesson Test 18		
Lesson Test 7			Lesson Test 19		
Lesson Test 8			Lesson Test 20		
Lesson Test 9			Lesson Test 21		
Lesson Test 10			Lesson Test 22		
Lesson Test 11			Lesson Test 23		
Lesson Test 12			Lesson Test 24		

Teacher name _____   Grade/Class _____

Student name	Pretest Score	Posttest Score	Percent Change (+/−)

Answer Keys

Pretest

Part 1: Vocabulary

1. c
2. a
3. d
4. b
5. d
6. c
7. a
8. b
9. d
10. b
11. c
12. a

Part 2: Grammar

13. c
14. d
15. b
16. a
17. c
18. b
19. d
20. a
21. c
22. c
23. b
24. d

Part 3: Reading and Writing

25. b
26. c
27. d
28. a
29. b
30. c
31. d
32. c
33. a
34. c
35. b
36. d

Lesson Test 1: The Reading Process

1. d
2. b
3. c
4. c
5. b
6. a

Lesson Test 2: The Writing Process

1. a
2. b
3. d
4. c
5. b
6. d

Lesson Test 3: Active Reading

1. c
2. a
3. d
4. b
5. c
6. a

Lesson Test 4: Understanding Sentences

1. a
2. c
3. b
4. c
5. d
6. b

Lesson Test 5: Reading Paragraphs

1. b
2. c
3. d
4. a
5. a
6. d

Lesson Test 6:
Ways of Organizing Paragraphs

1. d
2. c
3. b
4. d
5. a
6. c

Lesson Test 7: Descriptive Paragraphs

1. b
2. d
3. c
4. b
5. a
6. c

Lesson Test 8: Understanding Nouns

1. d
2. d
3. a
4. a
5. b
6. c

Lesson Test 9:
Reading an Autobiography

1. c
2. a
3. d
4. c
5. a
6. b

Lesson Test 10:
Reading Graphics and Websites

1. b
2. d
3. c
4. b
5. a
6. c

Lesson Test 11:
Writing an Expository Paragraph

1. c
2. b
3. a
4. d
5. c
6. b

Lesson Test 12: Understanding Verbs

1. b
2. c
3. d
4. b
5. a
6. c

Lesson Test 13: Reading Textbooks

1. b
2. d
3. a
4. d
5. b
6. c

Lesson Test 14: Reading Tests

1. c
2. a
3. c
4. d
5. b
6. b

Lesson Test 15: Writing Reports

1. b
2. d
3. a
4. c
5. a
6. b

Lesson Test 16: More About Verbs

1. d
2. a
3. b
4. c
5. c
6. d

Lesson Test 17: Reading a Story

1. c
2. d
3. b
4. a
5. d
6. c

Lesson Test 18: Writing a Narrative Paragraph

1. c
2. b
3. c
4. a
5. d
6. b

Lesson Test 19: Writing a Story

1. d
2. c
3. b
4. d
5. a
6. b

Lesson Test 20: Understanding Adjectives and Adverbs

1. b
2. a
3. c
4. d
5. c
6. b

Lesson Test 21: Reading Real-world Writing

1. b
2. a
3. c
4. a
5. d
6. b

Lesson Test 22: Persuasive Writing

1. c
2. a
3. b
4. c
5. d
6. b

Lesson Test 23: Writing Letters

1. d
2. c
3. a
4. d
5. b
6. a

Lesson Test 24: More Parts of Speech

1. b
2. c
3. d
4. d
5. b
6. a

Posttest

Part 1: Vocabulary

1. d
2. b
3. c
4. a
5. b
6. c
7. b
8. a
9. b
10. d
11. a
12. d

Part 2: Grammar

13. d
14. b
15. c
16. a
17. b
18. a
19. c
20. b
21. d
22. c
23. a
24. b

Part 3: Reading and Writing

25. c
26. a
27. d
28. c
29. d
30. b
31. a
32. c
33. b
34. a
35. d
36. d

Pretest

Part 1: Vocabulary

DIRECTIONS: Read each sentence. Choose the word that best fits in the blank. Fill in the bubble.

Sample

The cat sits on the _____.

(a) bike
(b) table
(c) ball
(d) story

---

1 Sandra has three _____ about Ellis Island.

(a) details
(b) strategies
(c) texts
(d) purposes

2 That bridge _____ two states.

(a) connects
(b) modifies
(c) organizes
(d) highlights

3 Amy _____ her story to make the story better.

(a) inherits
(b) baptizes
(c) collects
(d) revises

4 China is Jim's _____ land.

(a) specific
(b) native
(c) dependent
(d) singular

5 Please put the milk in the _____.

(a) clause
(b) judgment
(c) inference
(d) refrigerator

GO ON

Vocabulary

6 These are examples of _____.

ⓐ capitalization

ⓑ fragments

ⓒ punctuation

ⓓ testimony

7 She can _____ her new home.

ⓐ visualize

ⓑ admire

ⓒ require

ⓓ evaluate

8 Baseball is the _____ of this book.

ⓐ location

ⓑ subject

ⓒ exclamation

ⓓ scene

9 Randall _____ the book before he buys it.

ⓐ expands

ⓑ challenges

ⓒ remembers

ⓓ previews

10 Mrs. James writes the names in _____ order.

ⓐ helping

ⓑ alphabetical

ⓒ plural

ⓓ chronological

11 Holidays and birthdays are big _____ in your life.

ⓐ sources

ⓑ verbs

ⓒ events

ⓓ authors

12 The dragon is the only _____ creature in the book; the other animals are real.

ⓐ imaginary

ⓑ selective

ⓒ vertical

ⓓ interrogative

STOP

Name _____ Date _____

DIRECTIONS: Read each sentence. Choose the word that best fits in the blank. Fill in the bubble.

Sample

Mr. Ito _____ my teacher.

(a) is
(b) are
(c) have
(d) being

13 Canada and the United States are large _____.

(a) country
(b) countrys
(c) countries
(d) countryes

14 A pony is _____ than a horse.

(a) short
(b) shortest
(c) shortly
(d) shorter

15 Then Paco _____ the ball into the net.

(a) kick
(b) kicked
(c) kicking
(d) kicker

16 She parked the car _____ two buildings.

(a) between
(b) under
(c) through
(d) after

17 Jimmy _____ that window yesterday.

(a) break
(b) breaks
(c) broke
(d) breaked

GO ON

Grammar

18 Marcus and Betty go to work together. _____ ride the subway.

ⓐ He
ⓑ They
ⓒ We
ⓓ Them

19 She washed the teacup _____.

ⓐ careful
ⓑ carefuller
ⓒ carefullest
ⓓ carefully

20 We saw _____ in the sky.

ⓐ a bright star
ⓑ a star bright
ⓒ a brightly star
ⓓ a stars bright

21 Do you want the apple _____ the pear?

ⓐ but
ⓑ if
ⓒ or
ⓓ so

22 Joanne and I _____ on the telephone.

ⓐ am talking
ⓑ is talking
ⓒ are talking
ⓓ talks

23 The _____ desk is clean.

ⓐ teacher
ⓑ teacher's
ⓒ teachers'
ⓓ teachers's

24 The big yellow house, _____ my grandfather built, was sold yesterday.

ⓐ who
ⓑ where
ⓒ that
ⓓ which

STOP

Part 3: Reading and Writing

DIRECTIONS: Choose the best answer to each question. Fill in the bubble.

25 The first step in the writing process is Prewriting. What is the second step?

   (a) Edit and proofread

   (b) Write a draft

   (c) Publish and present

   (d) Revise the draft

26 Which of these is a complete sentence?

   (a) On a beautiful day in the middle of August.

   (b) A ship came into view many people stood on the deck.

   (c) The huge ship sailed into San Francisco Bay.

   (d) Past the Golden Gate Bridge and Alcatraz Island.

27 Which sentence is an <u>exclamation</u>?

   (a) Did you see that turtle?

   (b) It was sleeping in the sun.

   (c) Put the turtle in the water.

   (d) What a big snapping turtle!

28 What kind of literature is a true story about a person's life written by that person?

   (a) autobiography

   (b) essay

   (c) realistic fiction

   (d) editorial

29 What is the <u>setting</u> of a story?

   (a) a person or animal that takes part in the story

   (b) where and when the story takes place

   (c) what happens at the end of a story

   (d) the message or lesson taught in the story

30 Which of these is a proper noun?

   (a) a science teacher

   (b) the new book

   (c) Sandra Cisneros

   (d) next month

31 **Ramon must write a report about art for school. What should Ramon do first?**

ⓐ Organize the details.

ⓑ Write a draft.

ⓒ Make a bibliography.

ⓓ Choose a topic.

32 **Which of these is an example of persuasive writing?**

ⓐ friendly letter

ⓑ bus schedule

ⓒ political speech

ⓓ realistic fiction

Read the paragraph. Then answer questions 33–36.

Pearl Buck was an American writer. She was born in West Virginia in 1892. Her parents took her to China when she was young. Pearl went to college in the United States. Then she returned to China and began to write books. In 1932, she wrote her best novel, *The Good Earth*. It tells a story of China. She wrote many novels and short stories. She also wrote some biographies and essays. In 1938, Pearl Buck won a Nobel Prize for literature. She died in 1973.

33 **What is the main idea of this paragraph?**

ⓐ Pearl Buck was an American writer.

ⓑ She was born in West Virginia in 1892.

ⓒ Her parents took her to China when she was young.

ⓓ Pearl went to college in the United States.

34 **What kind of order is used to organize this paragraph?**

ⓐ compare and contrast order

ⓑ order of importance

ⓒ time order

ⓓ cause and effect order

35 **What kind of paragraph is this?**

ⓐ descriptive   ⓒ narrative

ⓑ expository   ⓓ persuasive

36 **Which sentence from this paragraph makes a judgment?**

ⓐ Pearl went to college in the United States.

ⓑ Then she returned to China and began to write books.

ⓒ She wrote many novels and short stories.

ⓓ In 1932, she wrote her best novel, *The Good Earth*.

Score

Number Correct	Percent Score
36	

Name _____ Date _____

Lesson Test 1: The Reading Process

DIRECTIONS: Choose the best answer to each question. Fill in the bubble.

1 The baker follows a <u>process</u> for making bread. What is a <u>process</u>?

   ⓐ lands ruled by one leader   ⓒ small parts of a whole

   ⓑ a set of paper notes   ⓓ a series of steps or actions

2 What should you do before reading?

   ⓐ Make connections between the story and your life.

   ⓑ Set a purpose for reading.

   ⓒ Pause and reflect on the poem, novel, or article.

   ⓓ Write in your reading journal.

3 What should you do after you read to help you understand a text?

   ⓐ Preview the selection carefully. ⓒ Take time to pause and reflect.

   ⓑ Use sticky notes to write ideas. ⓓ Figure out a strategy or plan.

4 What is the most important reason to learn about the reading process?

   ⓐ It gives you something to write down after you finish reading.

   ⓑ You can use it every time you read.

   ⓒ It can help you understand and remember what you read.

   ⓓ You might have a test on the reading process.

5 How can a Sequence Chart help explain the reading process?

   ⓐ It is a way to read the text again.

   ⓑ It shows the steps in the correct order.

   ⓒ It lists important things to think about.

   ⓓ It shows what you learned from reading.

6 Look at the quote from one student's reading journal. Which note shows the student making a personal connection to the quote?

Quote	Connection
"I am Chinese, but I am also American. I am both."	

   ⓐ I know how she feels. Since we left home, I am part of two cultures, too.

   ⓑ The writer is both Chinese and American.

   ⓒ The writer does not even know if she is Chinese or American!

   ⓓ I do not know anything about China.

Score

Number Correct	Percent Score
6	

Lesson Test 2: The Writing Process

DIRECTIONS: Choose the best answer to each question. Fill in the bubble.

1 I often use a dictionary when I am <u>editing</u>. What does the word
editing mean?
ⓐ correcting to use the right words and good sentences
ⓑ sharing or displaying work in front of others
ⓒ putting ideas into groups to make them clear
ⓓ thinking of many possible ideas

2 What is part of the prewriting step in the writing process?
ⓐ proofread   ⓒ write freely
ⓑ gather information   ⓓ check spelling

3 What should you think about before you start writing?
ⓐ publishing your work   ⓒ looking on the Internet
ⓑ showing your paper to others ⓓ your audience and purpose

4 Look at the web. What word best fits in the web?

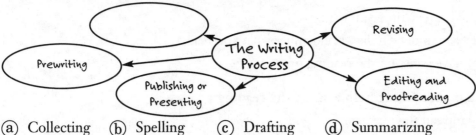

ⓐ Collecting   ⓑ Spelling   ⓒ Drafting   ⓓ Summarizing

5 What is the best way to organize the ideas in your draft?
ⓐ Write freely.
ⓑ Create a strong beginning, middle, and ending.
ⓒ Include descriptive details.
ⓓ Use a Revising Checklist to check your writing.

6 Look at the important information listed in the Summary Organizer.
What goes in the Subject box?

Subject: _____	
Important Information:	
1. Check spelling.	
2. Check for complete sentences.	
3. Check punctuation.	
4. Check capitalization.	

ⓐ Organize Details   ⓒ Grammar
ⓑ Writing Process   ⓓ Edit and Proofread

Score

Number Correct	Percent Score
6	

Lesson Test 3: Active Reading

DIRECTIONS: Choose the best answer to each question. Fill in the bubble.

1 I can <u>visualize</u> the ship he describes. What does <u>visualize</u> mean?

ⓐ show how things are alike   ⓒ make pictures in your mind

ⓑ call attention to something   ⓓ explain or give evidence

2 What should you do to become an active reader?

ⓐ think about what you read   ⓒ read with a partner

ⓑ make good decisions   ⓓ read about people like you

3 What is one way to be an active reader?

ⓐ count the words   ⓒ sing a song

ⓑ choose good books   ⓓ take notes

4 Which of these can best be used to compare and contrast two articles?

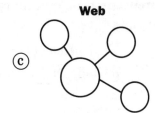

Double-Entry Journal

ⓐ
Quote	My Thoughts

Web

ⓒ

Venn Diagram

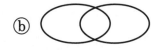

ⓑ

Inference Chart

ⓓ
Text	What I Conclude

5 Which of these is an example of "close reading"?

ⓐ Luis reads an exciting story quickly to find out what happens.

ⓑ Cho reads a funny note from her friend and laughs.

ⓒ Tina reads a poem slowly and carefully, word by word.

ⓓ Max reads the label on a cereal box to see what is in the cereal.

6 What is one good way to respond to a text?

ⓐ think about how it connects to your life

ⓑ use sticky notes to cover unimportant words

ⓒ agree with most of the author's ideas

ⓓ read another book as soon as you can

Score

Number Correct	Percent Score
6	

Name _____   Date _____

Lesson Test 4: Understanding Sentences

DIRECTIONS: Choose the best answer to each question. Fill in the bubble.

1 Tía Cristina made a loud <u>exclamation</u>. What is an <u>exclamation</u>?

  (a) a sudden, strong outcry   (c) a sentence that is a question

  (b) a command or request   (d) two sentences that run together

2 Which of these is a complete sentence?

  (a) Many of the people in   (c) Grandma wrote a letter to me.
      my family.

  (b) Using red, blue, or green ink.   (d) When he read the long letter.

3 Read the sentence. Which part is the <u>simple subject</u>?

  <u>Dark</u> <u>gray</u> <u>clouds</u> <u>floated</u> <u>in the sky.</u>
      (a)   (b)   (c)   (d)

4 Read the sentence. What sentence part is underlined?

  <u>Before we ate lunch</u>, we washed our hands.

  (a) phrase   (c) dependent clause

  (b) predicate   (d) independent clause

5 Which is a compound sentence?

  (a) Mr. Green grows corn and tomatoes in his garden.

  (b) Both corn and tomatoes need plenty of sun.

  (c) At the end of the summer, he picks the corn.

  (d) The tomatoes are red, but the corn is not ripe.

6 Look at the Details and Statement Organizer. What goes in the oval for "Broad Statement"?

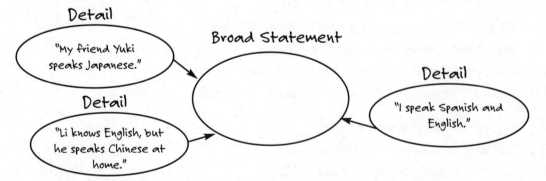

Detail
"My friend Yuki speaks Japanese."

Broad Statement

Detail
"I speak Spanish and English."

Detail
"Li knows English, but he speaks Chinese at home."

  (a) I speak two languages.

  (b) The students in my class speak many different languages.

  (c) Tatyana and her mother speak Russian.

  (d) Yesterday Li taught me the Chinese word for "friend."

Score	
Number Correct	Percent Score
	6

Name _____ Date _____

Lesson Test 5: Reading Paragraphs

DIRECTIONS: Choose the best answer to each question. Fill in the bubble.

1 Ricardo picked an interesting <u>topic</u>. What is a <u>topic</u>?

   ⓐ a conclusion ⓑ a subject   ⓒ a special time   ⓓ a key word

2 What does every paragraph tell about?

   ⓐ a funny joke ⓑ a sad story   ⓒ a main idea   ⓓ a true fact

Read the paragraph. Use the Main Idea Organizer to answer questions 3 and 4.

Ivan lives in the house beside us. I see him all the time. This year we are not in the same class, but we walk to school together every day. On the way, we talk about baseball, computer games, and comic books. Ivan tells a lot of jokes, and he always makes me laugh. If I have a problem, I tell Ivan. He listens and understands.

Main Idea:	
Important Details	**Unimportant Details**

3 What goes in the box for "Main Idea"?

   ⓐ We talk about baseball.   ⓒ I have a problem.

   ⓑ Ivan tells a lot of jokes.   ⓓ Ivan is my best friend.

4 What goes in the box for "Unimportant Details"?

   ⓐ Ivan is not in my class this year. ⓒ Ivan makes me laugh.

   ⓑ Ivan and I walk to school together. ⓓ Ivan listens to my problems.

Read the paragraph to answer questions 5 and 6.

(1) Renata had no sisters or brothers, but she was never lonely. (2) Nine of her cousins lived on her street. (3) Three aunts welcomed her into their kitchens for a quick snack or a long talk several times a week. (4) Grandma and Grandpa lived in the apartment upstairs. (5) Then everything changed. (6) When Renata was 13, she and her parents moved far away.

5 Which sentence gives the main idea of this paragraph?

   ⓐ Sentence 1   ⓑ Sentence 2   ⓒ Sentence 3   ⓓ Sentence 4

6 What inference can you make about Renata?

   ⓐ Renata did not like her aunts.

   ⓑ A lot of Renata's relatives lived nearby.

   ⓒ Renata wished she had a brother or a sister.

   ⓓ After Renata moved, she felt lonely for the first time.

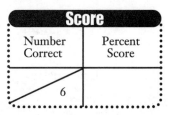

© Great Source. Copying is permitted; see page 2.

Name _____ Date _____

DIRECTIONS: Choose the best answer to each question. Fill in the bubble.

1 Ana wants to <u>organize</u> those pictures. What does the word <u>organize</u> mean?

ⓐ show how things are alike

ⓑ see something in your mind

ⓒ add to or help make stronger

ⓓ put together in a way that makes sense

2 Which of these are <u>signal words</u> that tell what happens in time order?

ⓐ because, why, as a result

ⓑ he, they, them

ⓒ first, then, after

ⓓ alike, different, same

3 Suki writes a paragraph. Details in the paragraph tell *why* something happened. What kind of order does she use in the paragraph?

ⓐ time order

ⓑ cause and effect order

ⓒ location order

ⓓ order of importance

4 Felipe wants to visualize the details of a paragraph that uses location order. Which step can help him visualize?

ⓐ Put important ideas in a web.

ⓑ Make a Venn diagram.

ⓒ Make a timeline.

ⓓ Draw a map or picture.

Think about watching TV and going to a movie theater. How are these things alike? How are they different? Use the Venn diagram to answer questions 5 and 6.

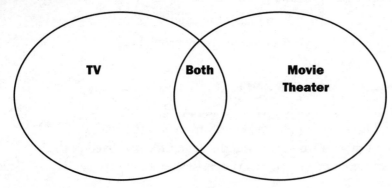

5 What goes under "TV"?

ⓐ stay home

ⓑ go with friends

ⓒ big screen

ⓓ buy popcorn

6 What goes under "Both"?

ⓐ small screen

ⓑ buy a ticket

ⓒ fun to watch

ⓓ many people

Score	
Number Correct	Percent Score
6	

Name _____ Date _____

DIRECTIONS: Choose the best answer to each question. Fill in the bubble.

1 The <u>scene</u> of the story is an old castle on a dark night. What is a <u>scene</u>?

  (a) what the writer says about a subject

  (b) the place where something happens

  (c) a change in something caused by the weather

  (d) a statement used as proof

2 Which phrase uses a *strong* adjective?

  (a) a good day   (c) nice trees

  (b) a lot of kids   (d) fluttering leaves

3 What does a descriptive paragraph use to help the reader see, hear, feel, smell, or taste something?

  (a) action verbs   (c) sensory images

  (b) a main idea   (d) signal words

4 Read the paragraph about a bike. Which detail helps you visualize the bike?

  Carmen looked at the bicycle in the store window. The bike was shiny red with silver stripes. A big sign on the bike said "Sale—$100!" Carmen really wanted that bike.

  (a) It was in the store window.   (c) The sign said "Sale—$100!"

  (b) It was shiny red with silver stripes.   (d) Carmen really wanted to buy it.

5 Look at the web. What goes in the oval to complete the web?

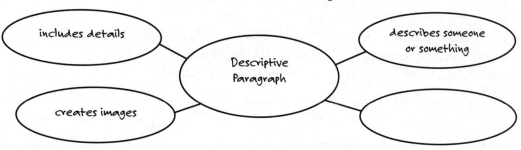

includes details

creates images

Descriptive Paragraph

describes someone or something

  (a) has a main idea   (c) has order of importance

  (b) has cause and effect   (d) has pictures and maps

6 Which detail best helps the reader visualize a baby?

  (a) The baby had a nice smile.

  (b) The baby looked cute.

  (c) The baby's mouth was shaped like an "O."

  (d) The baby was very small.

Score	
Number Correct	Percent Score
	6

Name _____ Date _____

DIRECTIONS: Choose the best answer to each question. Fill in the bubble.

1 **That word is an <u>irregular</u> verb. What does <u>irregular</u> mean?**

   ⓐ naming one   ⓒ definite or particular

   ⓑ belonging to someone;   ⓓ does not follow the rule; unusual
       possessive

2 **Read the sentence. Which word is a noun?**

We <u>were</u> a little <u>late</u> so we ran <u>to</u> catch the <u>bus</u>.
     ⓐ   ⓑ   ⓒ   ⓓ

3 **Which word is a plural noun?**

   ⓐ trees   ⓒ vegetable

   ⓑ sunshine   ⓓ Lincoln School

4 **Which sentence has correct capitalization?**

   ⓐ My friends and I play soccer every Saturday morning.

   ⓑ Irina lives on park street in Hadley.

   ⓒ Mrs. Lopez speaks spanish at home with her family.

   ⓓ *Tuck everlasting* is my favorite book.

5 **Choose the words that best fit in the sentence.**

Mr. Diego looked at the _____ and asked them to stay after class.

   ⓐ girl's homework   ⓒ girls homework

   ⓑ girls' homework   ⓓ girls's homework

6 **Read the paragraph about Chico. What goes in the oval to complete the web?**

    Chico measures the wood carefully and makes a mark with his pencil. He picks up the saw, but he does not cut yet. Instead, he puts down the saw and measures again. Then he cuts the wood. Chico checks his work and smiles. The cut is perfect.

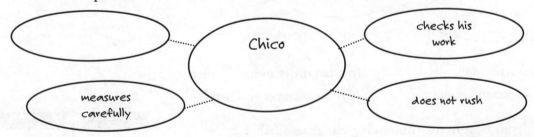

   ⓐ is 13 years old   ⓒ cares about his work

   ⓑ wears a red shirt   ⓓ enjoys a good book

Score

Number Correct	Percent Score
	6

Name _____ Date _____

Lesson Test 9: Reading an Autobiography

DIRECTIONS: Choose the best answer to each question. Fill in the bubble.

1 Yoshiko has different <u>views</u> about Japan. What are <u>views</u>?
ⓐ similar things in a row   © beliefs or opinions
ⓑ parts of a personality   ⓓ successes; accomplishments

2 What is a <u>biography</u>?
ⓐ a story about a person's life   © an article about important events
ⓑ a short news article   ⓓ a list of ideas

3 What are <u>key events</u> in an autobiography?
ⓐ a person's thoughts and ideas
ⓑ feelings or impressions that you form
© clear, descriptive adjectives
ⓓ important things that happened in a person's life

4 To understand how events in an autobiography shaped the author's life, what should you ask yourself?
ⓐ Is the author a foreigner?   © How did the author change?
ⓑ What is the author's age?   ⓓ Where does the author live?

5 To decide how you feel about the author of an autobiography, what should you do?
ⓐ Think about what the author says, does, and feels.
ⓑ Do the same things the author did.
© Memorize the series of events the author describes.
ⓓ Check to make sure the author's story is true.

6 Read the paragraph about Derek. Then choose the word that best completes the Character Trait Web.

Every Saturday morning, I ride my skateboard in the park. My skateboard is purple, and it says my name: "Derek Jones." One Saturday I started riding to the park. Then I saw a wallet on the sidewalk. The wallet was filled with money, and the owner's license was in it. The wallet belonged to Chang Li on Highland Street. I rode my skateboard to Highland Street and returned the wallet. Chang Li gave me $10 and put my picture in the newspaper.

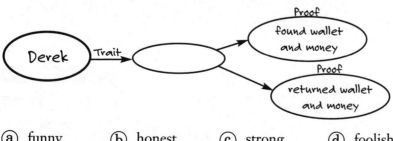

Score		
Number Correct	Percent Score	
	6	

ⓐ funny   ⓑ honest   © strong   ⓓ foolish

ACCESS *English* Assessments **27**

Name _____ Date _____

Lesson Test 10: Reading Graphics and Websites

DIRECTIONS: Choose the best answer to each question. Fill in the bubble.

1 Mrs. Gomez told us the <u>purpose</u> of the meeting. What is a <u>purpose</u>?
- (a) someone that gives information
- (b) a reason for doing something
- (c) a thing that represents something else
- (d) all the people in a place

2 What should you do first when you read graphics or websites?
- (a) Paraphrase the information.
- (b) Interpret the graphics.
- (c) Connect them to your own life.
- (d) Read all the words.

3 Look at the graphic. What is the graphic about?
- (a) number of students who go to the library
- (b) number of books sold each year
- (c) new books added to the King School library
- (d) students at the King School

New Library Books at King School 2001–2005

4 Which sentence best paraphrases the information in this graphic?

Languages Spoken at Home
by Oak School Students

- (a) Oak School students speak four different languages.
- (b) About half of Oak School students speak English at home.
- (c) Students at Oak School come from many countries.
- (d) Some Oak School students speak Russian.

5 What is the best way to find information on the Internet?
- (a) Use a search engine.
- (b) Ask a friend.
- (c) Make a line graph.
- (d) Use a paraphrase chart.

6 What is the best way to evaluate a website?
- (a) Look at the graphics to see if they are attractive.
- (b) See if it connects to your own life.
- (c) Check the source to see if it is reliable and up-to-date.
- (d) Ask yourself what you need to find out.

Score

Number Correct	Percent Score
	6

Name _____ Date _____

Lesson Test 11: Writing an Expository Paragraph

DIRECTIONS: Choose the best answer to each question. Fill in the bubble.

1 Mrs. Bono wrote a <u>series</u> of articles about the war. What is a <u>series</u>?

  (a) a collection of books or magazines

  (b) single items or facts about something

  (c) a number of similar things following one another

  (d) the work done to learn about a subject

2 An expository paragraph can be used to _____.

  (a) tell a joke   (c) tell a story

  (b) explain how to cook noodles   (d) describe a best friend

3 The words *first, next, before, later,* and *after* are signal words for _____.

  (a) time order   (c) location order

  (b) cause and effect   (d) comparison and contrast

Read the paragraph. Use the Cause-Effect Organizer to answer questions 4 and 5.

    During the night, a thunderstorm hit our area. It was so loud that my whole family woke up. Since we were all awake, we got up and watched the storm. Rain came down heavily, and branches blew in the wind. As a result, branches and leaves covered the yard this morning.

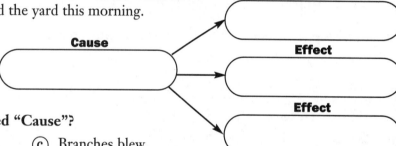

4 What goes in the oval marked "Cause"?

  (a) The family woke up.   (c) Branches blew.

  (b) Leaves fell into yard.   (d) A thunderstorm hit.

5 What goes in the oval for "Effect"?

  (a) during the night   (c) yard covered with leaves

  (b) the whole family   (d) was really loud

6 Read the paragraph. In time order, which event happened second?

    My grandmother had eleven brothers and sisters. When she was small, all of her family lived in Scotland. In 1904, her oldest brother came to America to find a job. Then, a year later, two more brothers needed jobs. They moved to Canada. Finally, by 1910, my grandmother saved enough money to leave Scotland, too. She settled in the United States.

  (a) Grandmother settled in the U.S.

  (b) Two brothers moved to Canada.

  (c) Oldest brother moved to U.S.

  (d) Grandmother left Scotland.

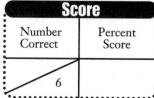

Score	
Number Correct	Percent Score
	6

Name _____ Date _____

Lesson Test 12: Understanding Verbs

DIRECTIONS: Choose the best answer to each question. Fill in the bubble.

1 **Passing the history test will <u>require</u> many hours of studying. What does <u>require</u> mean?**

  ⓐ tell when the action takes place

  ⓑ must have something; need

  ⓒ naming more than one person

  ⓓ have the same number

2 **Verbs are used to _____.**

  ⓐ tell what a subject is about

  ⓑ describe a person or place

  ⓒ show action or a state of being

  ⓓ name the topic

3 **Which sentence uses a verb in the *active voice*?**

  ⓐ Mario was woken up by his mother.

  ⓑ My hat was blown off by the wind.

  ⓒ A prize is given to the winning team.

  ⓓ Keiko plays the piano very well.

4 **Read the sentence. Which word is a helping verb?**

<u>This</u> afternoon Sammy <u>will</u> <u>cut</u> the grass for his <u>neighbor</u>.

  ⓐ   ⓑ ⓒ   ⓓ

5 **Which sentence uses verbs correctly?**

  ⓐ Daryl and Joseph are best friends.

  ⓑ Lin want a soccer ball for her birthday.

  ⓒ Nobody are staying late after school.

  ⓓ She and I is finishing our homework.

6 **Choose the word or words that best complete the sentence.**

Next June, my parents, my sister, and I _____ to Ann Arbor, Michigan.

  ⓐ am moving   ⓒ will move

  ⓑ moved   ⓓ have moved

© Great Source. Copying is permitted; see page 2.

Score

Number Correct	Percent Score
	6

30 *ACCESS English* Assessments

Lesson Test 13: Reading Textbooks

DIRECTIONS: Choose the best answer to each question. Fill in the bubble.

1 Luis <u>previews</u> the magazine before he buys it. What does the word <u>previews</u> mean?

   ⓐ asks questions about   ⓒ relates to one's life

   ⓑ looks at ahead of time   ⓓ brings back into the mind

2 What should you ask yourself to set a purpose for reading a textbook?

   ⓐ How many pages will I be reading?

   ⓑ What do I already know about this subject?

   ⓒ Do I need to take notes on my reading?

   ⓓ What do I need to learn or remember?

3 What should you do to preview a chapter in a textbook?

   ⓐ Look at headings, boldface terms, and graphics.

   ⓑ Read with a purpose.

   ⓒ Use the glossary and index to find information.

   ⓓ Take notes or make a web.

4 After reading a textbook chapter, a good way to remember what you learned is to _____.

   ⓐ make a plan   ⓒ connect to the reading

   ⓑ read the table of contents   ⓓ summarize the information

5 Richard wants to take Chapter Notes about a textbook. What should he do?

   ⓐ Write the topic in a circle and add details in circles around it.

   ⓑ Write the chapter headings and important details under each heading.

   ⓒ Write the events and dates in order with a description of each event.

   ⓓ Write the main idea of the chapter in a notebook.

6 Tatanya wants to compare and contrast the information about Abraham Lincoln in her textbook and her library book. Which is the best aid for her to use?

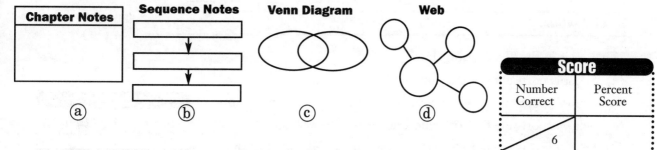

Name _____ Date _____

Lesson Test 14: Reading Tests

DIRECTIONS: Choose the best answer to each question. Fill in the bubble.

1 Nadia gathered information for a history <u>assignment</u>. What is an <u>assignment</u>?

   (a) a chapter in a textbook   (c) the work you must do for school

   (b) a conclusion made from facts   (d) a group of words that rhyme

2 Previewing a test can help you to _____.

   (a) make the best use of your time   (c) help you get ready for the test day

   (b) answer questions faster   (d) remember what you already know

3 The best way to answer inference questions is to _____.

   (a) use facts that you know to make a timeline

   (b) write an expository paragraph

   (c) put together what you read with what you already know

   (d) find the answer written in the passage

4 What important thing can you learn by looking closely at an essay question?

   (a) how to prepare for a test   (c) how to skim for key words

   (b) clues about the answer   (d) the topic of the essay

5 What is the best way to organize your thoughts and plan your response to an essay question?

   (a) Write quickly so you do not forget anything.

   (b) Make a graphic organizer.

   (c) Learn about the different kinds of test questions.

   (d) Circle the key words.

6 Look at the Evaluation Chart about school sports. Then answer the question.

Evaluation Chart

Subject: Evaluating the Importance of School Sports			
Detail Sports help make kids strong and healthy.	**Detail** Sports help kids make friends.	**Detail** Sports teach teamwork and cooperation.	**Detail** Sports help kids follow rules and directions.
Evaluation:			

What goes in the "Evaluation" box?

   (a) School sports are not that important.

   (b) School sports have several benefits, so they are very important.

   (c) School sports are fun for some students.

   (d) School sports are not needed for kids who are already healthy.

Score	
Number Correct	Percent Score
	6

Name _____ Date _____

Lesson Test 15: Writing Reports

DIRECTIONS: Choose the best answer to each question. Fill in the bubble.

1 Five students sat together to do some <u>brainstorming</u>. What is <u>brainstorming</u>?

ⓐ putting information in your own words

ⓑ thinking of many possible ideas

ⓒ writing words to tell about something

ⓓ listing all the references you used

2 Samuel chooses a topic for his report. What should he do next to start his research?

ⓐ Summarize the main points of the report.

ⓑ Create a bibliography for the report.

ⓒ Organize the details he wants to include.

ⓓ Make a list of questions to be answered.

3 Which of these can be used to organize information for writing a report?

ⓐ an outline   ⓒ a catalog

ⓑ a bibliography   ⓓ an index

4 When you write a report, what should the ending paragraph include?

ⓐ all the details that support the main idea

ⓑ the books used for research

ⓒ why this topic is important

ⓓ questions not answered in the report

5 Lisa wrote a report on railroads in America. What should she put in her bibliography?

ⓐ a magazine article she used for information

ⓑ the name of the library where she did her research

ⓒ an outline she used to organize details

ⓓ proofreader's marks used to edit the report

6 Julia made this Gathering Grid to help gather information for a report on the modern Olympic Games. What goes in boxes 2 and 3?

(1) **Subject: Olympic Games**	(2)	(3)
When did the Games begin?		
Where did the Games take place?		
Who competed in the Games?		

ⓐ main ideas   ⓒ other subjects

ⓑ sources of information   ⓓ questions to answer

Score

Number Correct	Percent Score
	6

© Great Source. Copying is permitted; see page 2.

ACCESS *English* Assessments **33**

Name _____ Date _____

Lesson Test 16: More About Verbs

DIRECTIONS: Choose the best answer to each question. Fill in the bubble.

1 Deanna looked for an example of a <u>suffix</u>. What is a <u>suffix</u>?

ⓐ a main idea   ⓒ a spelling test

ⓑ a concrete noun   ⓓ a word ending

2 Read the sentence. Which word is a helping verb?

Uncle Charles <u>has</u> <u>traveled</u> to <u>many</u> parts <u>of</u> the world.

       ⓐ   ⓑ   ⓒ   ⓓ

3 Which of these sentences uses a linking verb?

ⓐ Stan has dreamed about going to Guatemala.

ⓑ Maria is a talented artist.

ⓒ That boy loves to play baseball.

ⓓ Angela connected all the dots in the puzzle.

4 Which sentence uses the past participle of the verb *see*?

ⓐ I want to <u>see</u> the city of New Orleans.

ⓑ We are <u>seeing</u> many changes take place.

ⓒ She has <u>seen</u> the movie about Louis Armstrong.

ⓓ Last year I <u>saw</u> the Apollo Theater in Harlem.

5 Choose the word or words that best complete the sentence.

Timothy _____ seven straw hats for the fair last week.

ⓐ make   ⓑ is making   ⓒ made   ⓓ has made

6 Look at the Verb Chart. Which sentence goes under "Example" to demonstrate the verb *sing*?

Action Verb build sing tell	Example
Helping Verb is	Example

ⓐ That is my favorite <u>song</u>.   ⓒ My other trumpet is <u>missing</u>.

ⓑ Martin is a good <u>singer</u>.   ⓓ She <u>sang</u> "The Star-Spangled Banner."

Score	
Number Correct	Percent Score
	6

Lesson Test 17: Reading a Story

DIRECTIONS: Choose the best answer to each question. Fill in the bubble.

1 Carlo has a <u>conflict</u> at school. What is a <u>conflict</u>?

    ⓐ a surprise   ⓒ a problem or struggle

    ⓑ a turning point   ⓓ a time or place

2 Which of these is an example of fiction?

    ⓐ biography   ⓑ report   ⓒ news article ⓓ realistic story

Read this story. Then use the Fiction Organizer to answer questions 3–6.

Working Late

One summer morning, Miranda woke up early. She heard Papa talking in the kitchen. She quickly got out of bed and dressed.

"Good morning, Papa!" she said. She hugged her father and smiled. "I never see you anymore," she said quietly. "You work late every night and sleep all day."

"Yes," said Papa, "and I miss you very much. So, tonight you can come with me."

After dinner that night, Miranda got ready to go. Then she rode on the bus with Papa. They rode into downtown Sacramento and got off near a very tall building.

"This is where I work," Papa said, pointing up at the building. "Come with me. Tonight you can help me with my work."

Miranda smiled happily and said, "It is good to see you tonight, Papa!"

3 What goes in the box for "Characters"?

    ⓐ after dinner

    ⓑ Miranda and Papa

    ⓒ on the bus

    ⓓ Sacramento

4 What goes in the box for "Plot"?

    ⓐ A girl misses her father because he works all night.

    ⓑ A father gets a new job, and the family moves.

    ⓒ A girl gets out of bed and dresses for school.

    ⓓ A father goes on a long trip with his daughter.

5 What goes in the box for "Setting"?

    ⓐ at school

    ⓑ a very large house

    ⓒ working at night

    ⓓ the city of Sacramento

6 What goes in the box for "Theme"?

    ⓐ Tomorrow is another day.

    ⓑ Good friends are hard to find.

    ⓒ Make the best of what you have.

    ⓓ Traveling is fun.

Score

Number Correct	Percent Score
6	

Name _____ Date _____

DIRECTIONS: Choose the best answer to each question. Fill in the bubble.

1 A good story has <u>fluency</u>. What does the word <u>fluency</u> mean?

   ⓐ an unforgettable experience

   ⓑ a way of showing how to do something

   ⓒ an easy flow of ideas from one to the next

   ⓓ attention to choosing what is important

2 To write a narrative paragraph, what should you do first?

   ⓐ Make a checklist of traits.   ⓒ Gather information.

   ⓑ Choose a subject.   ⓓ Describe the characters.

3 Narrative paragraphs most often use what kind of order?

   ⓐ cause-effect order   ⓒ chronological order

   ⓑ order of importance   ⓓ location order

4 What is a writer's *voice*?

   ⓐ the writer's special way of telling a story

   ⓑ the sounds that words make

   ⓒ the conversation between characters in a story

   ⓓ a way to make writing sound true

Read this narrative paragraph. Then use the Story Organizer to answer questions 5 and 6.

When I was little, I liked to watch my mother make rugs. First my father drew a picture on a piece of burlap. Burlap is a plain fabric. Then my mother worked on each part of the picture. She used a hook and put colored strings on the rug. The strings came in many colors. When she was finished, she placed the rug on the floor. Every rug was so beautiful! We did not want to walk on them.

Beginning	Middle	End

5 What goes in the "Middle" box?

   ⓐ My father drew a picture.   ⓒ Burlap is a plain fabric.

   ⓑ I liked to watch my mother.   ⓓ My mother put strings on the rug.

6 What goes in the "End" box?

   ⓐ The strings came in many colors.

   ⓑ She placed the rug on the floor.

   ⓒ My mother worked on each part.

   ⓓ We sat on the rugs.

Score

Number Correct	Percent Score
6	

Name _____ Date _____

DIRECTIONS: Choose the best answer to each question. Fill in the bubble.

1 Greta has a nice <u>personality</u>. What does the word <u>personality</u> mean?

ⓐ the way someone looks

ⓑ a warm sweater

ⓒ a place to live

ⓓ the way someone acts or behaves

2 To write a story, what should you do first?

ⓐ Revise sentences.

ⓑ Describe the ending.

ⓒ Create the plot, setting, and characters.

ⓓ Think of a title for the story.

3 Which of these sentences describes a <u>setting</u>?

ⓐ Uncle Joe was a tall man with long white hair.

ⓑ He stood at the bus stop on Pine Street.

ⓒ Uncle Joe went to meet his nephew, Franny.

ⓓ They ate lunch and talked about many things.

4 In a story, you can use dialogue to _____.

ⓐ revise your sentences

ⓑ compare facts and opinions

ⓒ state the main idea

ⓓ make characters seem real

5 What is the next step after you revise your story?

ⓐ Edit and proofread.

ⓑ Read the story aloud.

ⓒ Make a Story Map.

ⓓ Write a draft.

6 Which of these can best be used to explain the events in a story?

ⓐ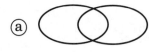

ⓒ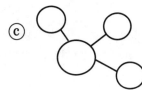

ⓑ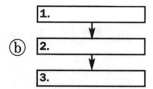

ⓓ Key Word | Notes

Score

Number Correct	Percent Score
6	

Name _____   Date _____

Lesson Test 20: Understanding Adjectives and Adverbs

DIRECTIONS: Choose the best answer to each question. Fill in the bubble.

1 Shem painted a <u>vertical</u> line on the wall. What does <u>vertical</u> mean?

   ⓐ in a funny way

   ⓑ straight up and down

   ⓒ wide and colorful

   ⓓ in the middle of a city

2 The <u>superlative</u> form of a word is used to _____.

   ⓐ compare three or more things

   ⓑ combine two sentences

   ⓒ name a person, place, or thing

   ⓓ show action

3 Which of these sentences uses an adverb?

   ⓐ Anna went to the grocery store.

   ⓑ That was the best sandwich in the world!

   ⓒ The painter finished the job quickly.

   ⓓ Miguel's car is bigger than Steve's.

4 Choose the word that best completes the sentence.

Jamal wears _____ sneakers to school every day.

   ⓐ very   ⓒ shoes

   ⓑ takes   ⓓ red

5 Choose the word that best completes the sentence.

Teva can draw pictures _____ than Lin can.

   ⓐ gooder   ⓒ better

   ⓑ best   ⓓ weller

6 Which is the best way to combine these two sentences?

> Joelle and I run through the park.
> The park is at the end of our block.

   ⓐ Joelle and I run through the park, and the park is at the end of our block.

   ⓑ Joelle and I run through the park at the end of our block.

   ⓒ At the end of our block, Joelle and I run through the park that is there.

   ⓓ Joelle and I run through the park it is at the end of our block.

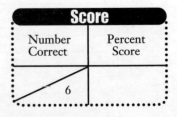

Score	
Number Correct	Percent Score
6	

Lesson Test 21: Reading Real-world Writing

DIRECTIONS: Choose the best answer to each question. Fill in the bubble.

1 This calendar has many nice <u>features</u>. What does the word <u>features</u> mean?

ⓐ reasons for doing something

ⓑ special parts or things that you notice

ⓒ steps that explain how to do something

ⓓ words or phrases that help you know what a word means

2 Which of these is an example of "real-world writing"?

ⓐ a bus schedule ⓑ a poem   ⓒ a play   ⓓ a comic book

3 To read real-world writing, what should you do first?

ⓐ Look for a plot, a setting, and characters.

ⓑ See how the information is organized.

ⓒ Decide on your purpose for reading.

ⓓ Talk and share with a friend.

4 When you read a schedule, which of these should you do?

ⓐ Skim to find just the information you need.

ⓑ Make a chart to keep track of the information.

ⓒ Take plenty of notes as you read.

ⓓ Use proofreader's marks to fix mistakes.

5 Which is the best tip for reading instructions?

ⓐ Make sure you have an encyclopedia handy.

ⓑ Make a list of sources right away.

ⓒ Put notes in order in a three-ring binder or file folder.

ⓓ Use a highlighter to mark important information.

6 Use the train schedule to answer the question.

Richmond, VA — Baltimore, MD				
Train Number		**98**	**84**	**82**
Days of Operation		**Daily**	**Mo–Fr**	**Sa**
Richmond, VA	DP	3:24A	6:05A	7:35A
Fredericksburg, VA	DP		7:00A	8:28A
Alexandria, VA	DP		7:52A	9:20A
Washington, DC	AR	5:45A	8:15A	9:45A
	DP		8:35A	10:20A
New Carrollton, MD	AR		8:46A	10:31A
Baltimore, MD	AR	6:44A	9:17A	11:02A

On Tuesday, what time does Train 84 arrive in Washington, D.C.?

ⓐ 5:45 A.M.   ⓑ 8:15 A.M.   ⓒ 8:35 A.M.   ⓓ 9:45 A.M.

Score

Number Correct	Percent Score
6	

Lesson Test 22: Persuasive Writing

DIRECTIONS: Choose the best answer to each question. Fill in the bubble.

1 Mr. Johnson looked at the <u>editorial</u>. What is an <u>editorial</u>?
- ⓐ a list of events in time order
- ⓑ a fact or supporting detail
- ⓒ an article that expresses an opinion
- ⓓ a person who works for a newspaper

2 The main purpose of persuasive writing is to _____.
- ⓐ change the way a reader thinks or acts
- ⓑ entertain the reader
- ⓒ compare and contrast two people or ideas
- ⓓ provide factual information on a topic

3 Which of these is one part of a good argument?
- ⓐ summary   ⓑ viewpoint   ⓒ setting   ⓓ character

4 Which of these is a key step in persuasive writing?
- ⓐ Make a list of helpful articles.
- ⓑ Find pictures to support your ideas.
- ⓒ Plan and organize your thoughts.
- ⓓ Ignore any opposing viewpoints.

5 Which of these sentences gives an opinion?
- ⓐ The County Fair will take place on September 10–12.
- ⓑ Last year more than 10,000 people went to the fair.
- ⓒ There will be contests, games, and races at the fair.
- ⓓ The County Fair is the best event of the summer.

6 Look at the Viewpoint and Evidence Organizer. Which answer best fits in the "Detail" box?

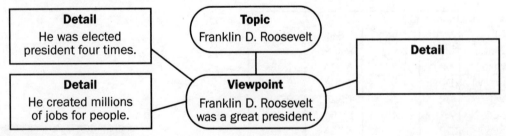

- ⓐ He was born near Hyde Park, New York, in 1882.
- ⓑ He led the U.S. to victory in World War II.
- ⓒ He enjoyed vacations in Warm Springs, Georgia.
- ⓓ He died when he was 63 years old.

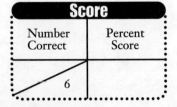

Score	
Number Correct	Percent Score
	6

Lesson Test 23: Writing Letters

DIRECTIONS: Choose the best answer to each question. Fill in the bubble.

1 Aunt Louise <u>sincerely</u> hopes you get well soon. What does <u>sincerely</u> mean?

ⓐ quickly   ⓑ in a silly way ⓒ nearly   ⓓ really; honestly

2 Whether you write a friendly letter, a formal business letter, or an email depends on which of these?

ⓐ how much time you have

ⓑ how persuasive you want to be

ⓒ your purpose and audience

ⓓ your salutation and signature

3 What kind of letter is this?

August 27, 2004

Dear Lucy,

   I am writing today from our new home. I like living here.

ⓐ a friendly letter   ⓒ a business letter

ⓑ an email to an editor   ⓓ a letter of complaint

4 Estevan wants to apply for a job. Which kind of letter should he write?

ⓐ a quick email

ⓑ a friendly letter

ⓒ a letter of opinion

ⓓ a formal business letter

5 A person who writes a letter of opinion is most likely to send it to _____.

ⓐ an aunt or uncle   ⓒ a best friend

ⓑ a newspaper   ⓓ a teacher

6 Which is the correct way to write the salutation in a business letter?

ⓐ Dear Mr. Miller: ⓒ Dear mr. miller:

ⓑ dear Mr. Miller   ⓓ Dear Mr. Miller,

Score

Number Correct	Percent Score
	6

Name _____ Date _____

Lesson Test 24: More Parts of Speech

DIRECTIONS: Choose the best answer to each question. Fill in the bubble.

1 Toya made a list of <u>conjunctions</u>. What is a <u>conjunction</u>?

  (a) a word that shows action

  (b) a word that connects groups of words in a sentence

  (c) a symbol used with numbers

  (d) a part of speech that shows strong emotion

2 Which of these uses a possessive pronoun?

  (a) We were very tired.

  (b) There is an oak tree near the house.

  (c) Dust covered their clothes.

  (d) Wow! They are amazing.

3 What is a good way to build your vocabulary?

  (a) Memorize the parts of speech.

  (b) Make an argument using viewpoint, detail, and opposing viewpoint.

  (c) Understand person, case, gender, and number.

  (d) Read every day and look up new words in a dictionary.

4 Which of these includes an interjection?

  (a) What did you say?   (c) Dear Isabel,

  (b) Please help me.   (d) Ow! That hurts.

5 Which sentence uses a prepositional phrase?

  (a) Mama went home early.

  (b) The firefighters climbed up the ladder.

  (c) Presidents give many speeches.

  (d) That is a big dictionary!

6 Look at the chart. What goes in the empty box under "Examples"?

Parts of Speech	Examples
Noun	car, house, apple
Verb	see, make, run
Preposition	

  (a) at, into, through

  (b) he, she, it

  (c) both, some, many

  (d) and, but, so

Score	
Number Correct	Percent Score
	6

Posttest

Part 1: Vocabulary

DIRECTIONS: Read each sentence. Choose the word that best fits in the blank. Fill in the bubble.

Sample

The cat sits on the _____.

(a) bike

(b) table

(c) ball

(d) story

1 We read this _____ about California.

(a) axis

(b) process

(c) grammar

(d) selection

2 My grandfather _____ old newspapers.

(a) infers

(b) collects

(c) challenges

(d) visualizes

3 Jaime uses a yellow pen to _____ important words.

> Many different groups of Native Americans lived in America. The Sioux lived on the Great Plains.

(a) inherit

(b) brainstorm

(c) highlight

(d) reread

4 Marisa looks for a _____ place on the map.

(a) specific

(b) broad

(c) dependent

(d) plural

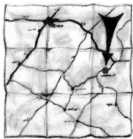

5 The name Alexander has four _____.

Al • ex • an • der

(a) purposes

(b) syllables

(c) details

(d) strategies

6 Gary Paulsen is the _____ of *Hatchet* and many other books.

    (a) outcome

    (b) fragment

    (c) author

    (d) conflict

7 The train from Boston _____ at 4:00 o'clock.

    (a) summarizes

    (b) arrives

    (c) skims

    (d) organizes

8 The river is part of the first _____ in this movie.

    (a) scene

    (b) mixture

    (c) cause

    (d) research

9 Lindsay likes to _____ math problems.

$$854 \div 17 = ?$$

    (a) reflect

    (b) solve

    (c) modify

    (d) embarrass

10 Mr. Parker makes a list of dates in _____ order.

    (a) major

    (b) alphabetical

    (c) narrow

    (d) chronological

February 12
March 15
April 1
May 31

11 Boris played a _____ of seven games of chess.

    (a) series

    (b) legend

    (c) population

    (d) passage

12 When Ellen plans the trip, everything goes _____.

    (a) glamorous

    (b) sincerely

    (c) complicated

    (d) smoothly

THINGS TO DO
- pack tent ✔
- bring food ✔
- bring flashlight ✔
- pack batteries

(STOP)

Name _____ Date _____

DIRECTIONS: Read each sentence. Choose the word that best fits in the blank. Fill in the bubble.

Sample

Mr. Ito _____ my teacher.

ⓐ is
ⓑ are
ⓒ have
ⓓ being

13 There are two _____ in the carriage.

ⓐ baby
ⓑ babys
ⓒ babyes
ⓓ babies

14 This book is _____ than yours.

ⓐ thick
ⓑ thicker
ⓒ thickest
ⓓ thickly

15 Bianca _____ in the show last Saturday.

ⓐ dance
ⓑ dances
ⓒ danced
ⓓ dancing

16. Benny jumped _____ the pool.

ⓐ into
ⓑ around
ⓒ under
ⓓ through

17 Amanda and her brother _____ a sand castle.

ⓐ builds
ⓑ built
ⓒ builded
ⓓ building

GO ON

Grammar

18 Caroline has three dogs. _____ walks them every day.

ⓐ She
ⓑ They
ⓒ Her
ⓓ Them

19 Grandpa smiled _____ when he saw the cake.

ⓐ happy
ⓑ happier
ⓒ happily
ⓓ happiest

20 A _____ sat on the branch.

ⓐ bird beautiful
ⓑ beautiful bird
ⓒ bird's beautiful
ⓓ beautiful birds'

21 It was raining, _____ I took my umbrella.

ⓐ or
ⓑ if
ⓒ then
ⓓ so

22 Theo and I _____ for the bus.

ⓐ am waiting
ⓑ is waiting
ⓒ are waiting
ⓓ waits

23 My _____ truck is filled with tools.

ⓐ father's
ⓑ father
ⓒ fathers
ⓓ fathers'

24 The apple pie _____ I baked yesterday is gone.

ⓐ which
ⓑ that
ⓒ there
ⓓ who

STOP

Part 3: Reading and Writing

DIRECTIONS: Choose the best answer to each question. Fill in the bubble.

25 **What is the last step in the writing process?**

ⓐ Edit and proofread.

ⓑ Write a draft.

ⓒ Publish and present.

ⓓ Revise the draft.

26 **Which of these is a complete sentence?**

ⓐ Glenna goes to the grocery store by herself.

ⓑ At 3:00 o'clock when she gets to the store.

ⓒ A gallon of milk, a loaf of bread, and some cheese.

ⓓ She buys some fish she will bake it for dinner.

27 **Which of these is an imperative sentence?**

ⓐ Did you paint your house?

ⓑ What a beautiful color!

ⓒ There are two cans of paint left.

ⓓ Be careful with that paintbrush.

28 **What kind of literature tells a made-up story that could happen?**

ⓐ autobiography

ⓑ essay

ⓒ realistic fiction

ⓓ editorial

29 **What is the theme of a story?**

ⓐ a person or animal that takes part in the story

ⓑ where and when the story takes place

ⓒ what happens at the end of a story

ⓓ the message or lesson taught in the story

30 **Which of these is a proper noun?**

ⓐ my country

ⓑ New Jersey

ⓒ a history book

ⓓ the governor

GO ON

31 Mariah must write a persuasive speech about volunteering in the community. What should Mariah do first?

ⓐ Form an opinion.

ⓑ Write a draft.

ⓒ Gather supporting details.

ⓓ Edit and proofread.

32 What kind of letter should you write to apply for a summer job?

ⓐ a friendly letter

ⓑ a letter of opinion

ⓒ a business letter

ⓓ a letter of complaint

Read the paragraph. Then answer questions 33–36.

Canada and Mexico are both neighbors of the United States, but they are very different countries. Mexico has hot weather, but many parts of Canada are cold. In Mexico, most people speak Spanish. In Canada, most people speak English or French. There are 103 million people in Mexico, but only 32 million people live in Canada. However, Canada is much larger than Mexico and has more natural resources. Both Canada and Mexico are beautiful places to visit.

33 What is the main idea of this paragraph?

ⓐ Canada and Mexico are both neighbors.

ⓑ Canada and Mexico are very different countries.

ⓒ Mexico has hot weather, but many parts of Canada are cold.

ⓓ There are 103 million people in Mexico but only 32 million people in Canada.

34 What kind of order is used to organize this paragraph?

ⓐ compare and contrast order

ⓑ order of importance

ⓒ time order

ⓓ cause and effect order

35 What kind of paragraph is this?

ⓐ narrative

ⓑ persuasive

ⓒ response to literature

ⓓ expository

36 Which sentence from this paragraph makes a judgment?

ⓐ Mexico has hot weather, but many parts of Canada are cold.

ⓑ There are 103 million people in Mexico, but only 32 million people live in Canada.

ⓒ However, Canada is much larger than Mexico and has more natural resources.

ⓓ Both Canada and Mexico are beautiful places to visit.

Score

Number Correct	Percent Score
36	